SOUL AFFIRMATIONS

Affirmations to balance your mind, body & soul

The formula used in these affirmations is to
Identify any imbalance
Reform your emotional energy &
Empower you

Nancy Finch

Foreword

Nancy Finch, esteemed holistic therapist, healer and Reiki Master lives and works in Cornwall. With over 15 years of training, teaching and professional experience, Nancy's work has touched and changed the lives of countless individuals.

'Soul Affirmations', inspired by Nancy's very own life journey, is a book that has something for all of us. Affirmations enable us to change and take more control of our lives. They help us to alter old thought patterns, heal past hurts and take responsibility for the way we experience things.

The affirmations in here offer us food for the soul as we journey through life. They nourish and protect us as we experience challenges and change. They support and strengthen us as we address relationship difficulties or issues of self-confidence and worth and they inspire and empower us as we grow into ourselves and live our life more as we want it. The concepts and affirmations in here can help us to experience more truth, more abundance, more peace and more love.

'Soul Affirmations' is a life changing work. The words in here have provided inspiration and support not only to Nancy but to hundreds of her clients. Now they are shared in this powerful publication, a gift from Nancy for everyone's growth and enjoyment. *Emma Mansfield.*

Contents

How Affirmations Work

Affirmations are strong statements of positive intention used to rebalance our emotions and feelings. This in turn has a <u>positive effect on our general well-being</u>. We have to in fact "lie" (tell ourselves the complete opposite of what we are feeling) to draw to ourselves (like a magnet) the desired state of being. <u>The more we read</u> and take in these affirmations the <u>more likely they are to work.</u> Your subconscious doesn't know the difference between a truth and a lie, so an affirmation will help you to produce the thing you <u>say</u> it feels. The more difficult the affirmation is to say the better; this usually means that you really need the one that's hardest to read or experience. When we say what we want to feel through affirmations, we allow ourselves to <u>raise our energy to a higher place</u>. Your new place of energy then attracts only the good things into your life and you will soon see rewarding results. Another way of looking at your energy is to think of it as <u>like attracts like</u>. For example, if you think of your energy as a reflection of what you are feeling, when you feel low your energy is low. It's like projecting energy into the world like the light of a 20 watt bulb, so you're attracting into your life more of the 20 watt things and feelings. But when you are in a positive place in your emotions e.g. gratitude, then you are transmitting positive energy like the light of a 100 watt bulb, bringing into your life more 100 watt things and feelings. So, positive affirmations work to help us gain confidence and control over the things that dis-empower us. Affirmations also offer us a chance to change old belief habits. They give us hope when times are hard. They can inspire us and make us grow stronger, and lastly they help us to see our own power and potential in all that we are, and can be. Research has shown that if we keep our thoughts in a positive place then we increase our well-being, feel good and we are an inspiration to others.

'If you change the way you look at things, the things you look at change.' (Wayne Dyer). There are no limits to what you can achieve when you use your thoughts to serve your wishes. Simply think/feel what it is you wish to have or to experience and watch how quickly you draw these things into your life. Self judgment and your acceptance of abundance can make you feel "it can't be this easy" but we can rewrite old belief patterns. If you think of yourself as a flower, pot bound, your act of re-potting yourself allows you to receive "more" from life, and grow into the fully developed "beautiful flower" you deserve to be. Have fun growing with your affirmations to help you.

And know that: Happiness is your right.

<u>How to use this book</u>

There are four ways to use this book:

1. Look at the coloured image on the front of this book and the zones covering the body. If you have a physical imbalance or painful area anywhere on your body then you can simply identify the condition with the colour zone that you need to read. Open up that section relating to the imbalance and choose one or more of the ten affirmations that you feel is right for you - the affirmation that seems hardest to read is often the one you need most.

2. Open up the book at random and set your intention to ask/receive "what do I need today?"

3. Work through each of the affirmations. Start with the Red section and work your way upwards through to the Purple zone choosing one or more from each section each day.

4. If you are in a hurry or have little time available then just go to your chosen affirmation and read the part that is underlined. This part is intended to carry the most energy.

<u>Determination</u>

Today I look at the determination I use in my life. I see at times I need the energy of this "gift" to establish myself in my world, and without it I may lack the driving force to achieve my goals and ambitions. The self discipline, tenacity and strength that comes from my determination enables me to embrace my will-power to gain satisfaction and reward.

As I gracefully accept the achievements I focus on, <u>I feel gratitude for the "gifts" my determination brings to me</u>.

My Well-Being

Today I recognise, feel and celebrate my
well-being. I allow no illness or condition
to take it from me. I do everything I can
to care for my body. I recognise all
imbalances only to release them from me.
<u>I see myself as a fit and healthy person.</u>
<u>My energy serves me well</u>,
and I am able in all I set out to do.
At all times I am aware of my bodily needs
and I aspire to meet these needs.
Every imbalance serves me to a better
understanding of myself. As I discover my
healing power within me, I feel confident
of a full and happy life.

<u>Pain</u>

Today I am aware of both my physical and emotional pain. I draw attention to it only to release it from me, I recognise that my mind and body wants to heal itself; and that my painful imbalance is just a way of communicating the need for change in my life. I trust my body's sub-conscious message of pain as a part of the process to re-balance myself. With new understanding I awaken the process of healing within me. <u>Releasing all pain, I choose to both cleanse and restore myself to full health</u>.

Passion

Today I look at the passion I have in my life.
How is this powerful force serving me?
I realise that utilising passion opens me up
to positive change; and that I can achieve
amazing results when I use this driving
force to bring me what I want. What I feel
passionate about and focus on is the place
where my energy is well spent and
delivered. So today I am inspired and
energised by my passion for life.
<u>Everything I invest with passion;
rewards me with satisfaction</u>.

Pleasure

Today <u>I give myself permission to take
pleasure from my life</u>.
I am aware of my needs, and validate
my right to experience all
that life can offer me on this level.
I do not judge or excuse myself from
allowing the things that make me happy
and so with humble respect I choose to
indulge in the pleasures I was born to
receive. I show myself moderation so as
not to distort myself from my desire.
Pleasure is a food on which
I feed my body; my mind and my soul are
nourished as I find balance and harmony
in all my needs.

Safety and Protection

Today I choose to recognise and embrace a deep sense of safety and protection, and with this sense of safety emerges courage and support. I know if I can digest these feelings into my soul then I am able to move forward to new and exciting opportunities. I now feel ready to embrace new situations and feel no limit as to what I can do in my life. As I welcome and support my need for change, I also welcome a new found liberation that leads me to happiness and fulfilment.

Slowing Down

Today I am aware of how I need to slow down in my life. The demands I make on myself can make me run at a pace that disables me from truly enjoying the ground on which I stand. I know that as I slow down I am able to "smell the roses" and feel the connection I have with myself. So today, I reduce the speed at which I travel; use detachment from self pressure; and grant myself the mindfulness of the present moment.

<u>Slowing down allows me to take respite from my hectic world</u>.

Strength

Today I look at the strength I have in my life.
Where do I display this powerful "gift"?
I recognise that to embrace the full potential
of strength I need to identify where it is I
need it most. So today I choose to direct
my strength to a place of intent; embrace
the power I need to re-balance my life, and
to give myself the opportunity to be all I
can be. Strength is the driving force on
which I build my dreams.
I use strength to support and motivate
me to my full potential.

The Body

Today I choose to love this body
that carries my soul,
value and respect it -
pay attention to its needs
and stay grateful to it.
I am humbled by its vulnerability -
but I am not afraid
of its disabilities and restrictions,
I can overcome them
with the unconditional love
I show myself.

<u>Trying too hard</u>

Today I am aware of how I sometimes try too hard in life. The pressure I put on myself to achieve all I can be can become a drain on my much needed energy. How ironic it is that I find I am less able to be my true self as a result of trying too hard. Somewhere along the line I alter my perception of me. So today, I choose to celebrate my sense of "just being" in the moment; without reward or obvious satisfaction; I detach myself from outcome and expectations.
<u>As I free myself from trying too hard;
I push the "easy" button in life</u>.

Attachment

Today I look at my attachment to people, things and situations; all of which I realise are just illusions resulting in my emotional restriction. I examine my logic or need of this disabling condition in my life, and see that attachment involves my projection of ego or expectations onto something or someone; often leading to disappointment and despair. So today <u>I release my dependence and instead use courage to explore new ways of fulfilment</u>. The absence of attachment leads me to emotional wisdom and grace.

Boundaries

Today I look at the boundaries I set in my life. Am I validating myself enough to set boundaries with people and situations? If I find myself without self honour and respect, or feel violated by something or someone then it is probably due to the need of this "gift". To set my boundaries is to acknowledge the things I wish from others. So <u>today I use power and grace to enforce my boundaries to the world</u>; to understand and respect the boundaries of others; and to feel safe and satisfied in my world.

Breaking Down

Today I am aware of how my life's circumstances have at times broken down in order to be rebuilt and be better than before. Just as I would demolish an old building to establish the new, I see that I too have had many phases of my life where I have found myself having to break down what is no longer of use to me. New ground may cause me to feel insecure and uncertain of the way my life is going, but as I remind myself to follow the natural flow of life, I gain trust that all changes will lead me to where I need to be.

Comfort

Today I look at my need for comfort.
I am aware of how my mind and body need
this "gift". As a child I needed tender loving
care, and so it is that as an adult, I still need
the warmth and safety of all that comfort
brings. But to look to my world to fulfil my
needs may lead to frustration and despair.
So today I learn to comfort, nurture and
support myself in times of need. As I feed
myself the warmth I crave;
I embrace comfort as the strength on
which to build my happiness.

Desire

Today I look at my desire and all it
represents to me in my relationships,
possessions, and situations. I know that
anything I yearn for is an expression of my
hunger and passion made up into form.
Identified by my mind, and motivated by my
emotions, I use desire as the power I need to
achieve all I want. While I anticipate
reward, I am cautious to use this force
with care so as not to distort my values.
As I embrace my desire,
I feel the excitement of being alive.

Friends

Today I celebrate my friends.
My gratitude and appreciation is surpassed
only by my love for them. I am humbled by
the unconditional warmth and support given
to me when life's challenges weaken me.
Friends remind me that I'm not alone; they
have been my salvation, my safety, my
comfort and my strength. My friends are the
family I choose. They listen to, validate and
respect who I am; I see a clear reflection of
myself in their eyes.
Friends lead me to higher ground;
from there I can see the stars.

Relationships

Today I look at my relationships; how do I feel within them? I know the reward and satisfaction they bring but I also know the pain. So today I recognise that all my relationships are just mirrors of me; who I am and need to become is reflected in the eyes of the people I know.
I am objective about my emotional feelings and reactions; presenting the opportunity for me to change, evolve and mature within my relationships.
<u>I take comfort and strength knowing that all relationships help me to know myself</u>.

Self Worth

Today I choose to see, feel and
celebrate my self worth.
I do not need another person to validate
my worth, or to feel that their attention
towards me gives me value or importance.
If I find myself affected by a lack
of self worth due to some
disappointment or self judgment, I will
quickly rebalance myself to respect and
value who I am. I do not have to justify
myself as a person that without satisfaction
has no worth. As I am able to see my own
worth, I can see the worth in others. I
embrace all situations to evolve me to an
unchanging sense of self worth.

Untangle Myself

Today I look at how I complicate my life;
like a ball of string with ends that need
unpicking. I need to undo any intense
feelings that deny me the elixir of life. To
untangle my emotional thinking and all that
it evokes me to feel; is to be patient, kind
and considerate to myself. I am eager to
untangle my life in the interest of balance,
and to find an uncomplicated and gracious
place within me. <u>As I learn to untangle
myself, I set myself free from the
heaviness of all that life can be</u>.

Value

Today I look at value in my life. How do I value myself and all that I've become? It is important for my emotional development to address myself to the honesty of this "gift" and to remember that by valuing myself without ego or self judgment, I am able to know my own truth without self righteous distortion. So today I choose to embrace value; not only to recognise my own virtues, but to be humbled by the value of others.

<u>As I embrace self value I gain honour, respect and appreciation for all that I am</u>.

<u>Anger and Remorse</u>

Today I recognise, feel and examine my own
feelings of anger and remorse. I understand
the need for anger as it has the power to
change my world. As I acknowledge this
power, <u>I see my anger as an opportunity to
take positive action for the change I need in
my life</u>. I allow the potential of happiness
to emerge from the intensity of my situation.
I embrace my feelings of remorse and
sadness only to use them in my new
understanding and support of myself.
As I take responsibility for my feelings, I
evolve to a stronger wiser self.

Detachment from Fear

Today I am aware of how fear can disable my ability to feel safe and happy in my life. I recognise this powerful emotion to be necessary at times, but held in my mind for too long it will distort and control my sense of well-being. And so <u>I choose to use detachment to control and rebalance my situation</u>. I allow myself distance from my intense reactions to fear, and in doing so find the wisdom to stay focused in the power of now. Being present in the moment allows me to welcome peace and happiness back into my life.

<u>Don't Take it Personally</u>

Today I recognise that I may be taking life
personally. I am aware of how people cause
me to react in a painful way. But with
detachment and understanding, I choose
not to take it personally, knowing that
<u>any injustice aimed towards me is simply
the other person's own pain personified</u>.
People react according to their own truth,
and so with understanding I
release my involvement from
the emotion that drives me to respond.
As I use detachment to separate myself from
my own reactions, I evolve to know new
strength and empowerment.

Energy

Today I am aware of the energy I need to enjoy in all areas of my life. I feel my mind and body are at their optimum best, and my objective in life is to meet all challenges with competence and ease.

<u>I use my energy wisely and see myself masterfully achieving all I need to do</u>.

I acknowledge my energy to be a driving force on which I can build my dreams. And so as I embrace this power, I enjoy motivation, achievement and satisfaction in my world.

My energy serves me well.

Free to Be Me

Today I am in touch with my feelings.
I support and value my decisions in life.
I have confidence and express myself with
ease. I know liberation is my right, and I
feel comfortable to expand my sense of self.
I release all negative emotions that have held
me back, and replace them with positive
feelings of purpose and trust.
As I follow my destiny, I find new strength
and dignity in all that I am.
I celebrate my right to be here and to
know my potential.
Today I am free to be me.

Frustration

Today I recognise my feelings of frustration. I understand my response to people and situations as my need to feel validated in my personal view. When situations drive me to react with frustration, I remind myself to step back a little from the cause, withhold my need for justice and use trust that I will eventually feel satisfied as a result of my patience and maturity. <u>As I move forward into a calm state of control I know frustration has no power over me unless I allow it to</u>. Liberation is mine.

Happiness Now

Today I see my future as a bright
and happy place to be. I
am able to ask for and accept
all that life can offer me.
My conviction to my dreams and
the love in my heart frees me
from fear and worry.
<u>I am happy now</u>.

My Power

Today I recognise, feel and celebrate my own power. I allow no-one to take it from me, and I do not give it away easily.
I recognise my right to be here in this world that knows my existence. I see myself as a whole person; my power serves me towards my highest good. At all times I feel safe and protected within my power.
Everything that happens to me leads me to my liberation and glory. As I discover and evolve my personal power, I inspire others to embrace theirs.
I use my power with wisdom and grace.

Playtime

Today I practice playtime. I know the value
of this pastime to be imperative to my state
of well-being. With new awareness,
I allow playtime into my busy life to
release the burden of my sensible self.
Embracing the satisfaction and delight that
this respite brings to me, I am able to restore
myself to a happier state of being. Well
deserved, this "gift" offers me time out from
the pressure and chaos that I choose to
create, freeing me to enjoy the sweet
nectar of fun in my life.

The Power of the Child

Today I acknowledge the power of the child. With amazement I see it's not just the obvious beauty or the form of innocence; but to witness a child experiencing the "in the moment" joy of all that life can be makes me realise that I may have lost this liberating energy as I have grown older, and replaced impulsiveness with purpose. So <u>today I choose to jump into puddles, go barefoot on the grass, and not to worry about the consequences</u>. As I re-connect to the power of the child within me I feel the "magic" of all that life can be.

Balance

Today I take a look at the way I balance my life. Am I spending more time in just one area? Or have I got the balance right? Maybe I have been working or playing too much. This imbalance could drain my energy and leave me feeling exhausted. So today <u>I choose to change where I place my energy, to bring myself back into harmony</u>, and to take action and responsibility for the equilibrium I aim to achieve. My life is greatly improved as I enjoy my new found state of balance.

<u>Family</u>

Today I look to my family with new found wisdom and grace. I feel my connection and celebrate its creation. <u>My love for my family is compounded by intense and intimate moments of truth that inspire me to new awareness and growth</u>. This truth confirms that whatever pain we unwillingly cause each other, love still remains the fundamental force that holds us together. With new value and appreciation, I grow stronger from knowing those I hold close to my heart. I am fortunate to know and love my family.

Forgiveness

Today I feel the need to embrace forgiveness. With deep awareness of past pain I choose to separate myself from the hurt that I've carried inside me, and instead hold a gentle view that all pain makes me grow stronger. There is no situation or person that can make me carry the burden of pain unless I allow it. So as I learn to use forgiveness I am healing myself on a deep level. My heart and soul now know a new state of serenity; freeing me to embrace forgiveness for others; but most of all for myself.

Gratitude

Today I am aware of my gratitude for everything wonderful in my life; the smile of a child, the kindness of a stranger, the wonders of nature all fill me with humble gratitude. How amazing life is when I look through these eyes, and how important it is to remember to look. As I focus on gratitude my heart fills with delight and wonder. <u>I feel the entirety of my soulful self; immersing into the light of all that brings me joy</u>. When I am grateful; I bring forth a state of happiness that puts a smile on my face and food in my soul.

<u>Grief and Sorrow</u>

Today I recognise and feel my pain and sorrow. I may not understand it or welcome it into my life, but instead I choose to know its power over me, and with this new understanding <u>I feel a sense of trust that I will evolve and grow stronger from all I feel</u>.

I recognise my need for comfort and support and learn to give myself the things I need from others. I am gentle, kind and patient with myself as I travel through this journey of awareness.

Every loss and sorrow leads me to a peaceful and liberated state of being.

Guilt and Self Judgement

Today I am aware of my feelings of guilt and self judgement. I know that these negative emotions are only my perception of past feelings, and so with compassion and understanding I choose to release the burden of them from my life. The power I feel in the present moment demands that <u>I do not have to justify myself, or allow guilt or self judgement to be detrimental to my well-being</u>.

With new strength and wisdom I embrace every situation as an opportunity for me to evolve. Emotional freedom is mine.

Loneliness

Today I am aware of my feelings of loneliness. I may long for company to comfort and fulfil my needs, or feel disabled by the void that keeps me from happiness but in my soul I know that I can give myself the things I need from others, and in reality I need only to recognise my own wholeness to be happy. Time alone offers many gifts. With new hope and understanding I embrace my time alone as an opportunity to evolve into a strong, independent and fulfilled person. <u>I may walk alone, but my heart knows happiness</u>.

<u>Love</u>

Today I believe I am loveable,
I deserve rewarding relationships
that bring me love and happiness.
Love is the answer to all my problems.
As I accept love into my life,
my whole world becomes a
wondrous place to be.
<u>I bask in the warmth of love</u>
<u>embracing all that it can offer me</u>.
Love is all.

Patience

Today I recognise my need for patience.
When I feel frustrated by the urgency of
something I want or need; then I suffer from
restricted energy. My attention is being spent
focusing and obsessing about my desires.

So today I re-adjust my focus, and use
maturity and self discipline to know that I
will eventually have satisfaction. As I honour
the stillness inside me, <u>I release my sense of
urgency, and trust that eventually I will have
happiness and fulfilment from knowing
patience</u>.

Peace

Today I recognise my need for peace. How often do I experience this wonderful "gift?" Not enough, as my hunger for it shows me. To keep a sense of harmony in my life, I need to recognise that peace is paramount in respect of my well-being, and that I need to gracefully set my intention to create this spiritual place of being. So today I indulge and commit myself to the serenity, happiness and equilibrium that peace can bring. With awareness I embrace a deep sense of peace in my world.

<u>Creativity</u>

Today I am aware of my creativity
I see that at times the flow of this "gift"
may have been restricted and in need of
liberation. So today I affirm to myself,
my powerful intention is to create
amazing results, and that
<u>everything I create flows
naturally and with ease</u>.
I have no boundaries, blocks or limits to
hold me back. So as I embrace my creative
freedom, I see rewarding results.
Fulfilment allows me to
enjoy all that my creativity creates.

<u>Dancing Butterflies</u>

Today I look to the butterflies I see dancing around me. They dance without a care; just in the moment, experiencing all that life can offer them. They remind me of how I too should dance in the moment with life. Here I have the chance of pure joy. I can have this liberation at any time; as long as <u>I focus on all the freedom giving moments and forget all else that steals it away from me</u>. How beautiful that moment is; when I draw my attention to the present. As I learn to dance like the butterflies; I feel the joy of all that life can be.

Expression

Today I choose to look at how I use my expression. I know in order to grow in my ability I have to open myself up to be liberated to my full potential. And so I explore new ways of expressing myself. I find freedom to "show myself" to the world without fear of the consequences. Whilst careful to use grace and consideration to others, I avoid any risk of bombastic expression. I know that <u>as I evolve into soulful expression, all areas of my life are improved</u>.

Honesty

Today I take a look at how I use honesty
in my life. I appreciate and value how
liberating and rewarding this wonderful
"gift" can be. And so I choose to give myself
permission to speak my truth without
compromise, to evolve to a more refreshing
state of being, and to know that
<u>honesty provides me with the opportunity
to keep council with myself</u>.
When I suffer the contamination of
falseness about me,
I use honesty to restore me to
emotional and spiritual health.

Hope

Today I acknowledge my need of hope. When times are hard and my energy is low, I may suffer discouragement from some form of "lack" in my life. Instead, I choose to use hope so that <u>no matter how hard life's challenges seem to be, all will be right in the end</u> and happiness will prevail. Hope re-introduces acceptance and patience at a time I need it most, leading me to perceive understanding and peace of mind. Hope is my promise of liberation,
happiness and
glory.

<u>Laughter</u>

Today I look at how much laughter
I have in my life. I recognise that I may not
laugh enough; and that I could be taking
myself too seriously. When I am sensible, I
connect to the light hearted energy
inside me that keeps me happy and well. So
<u>today I recognise the need to balance the
heaviness of my life with the "gift" of
laughter</u>. Changing my attitude is something
I can do at any given moment.
Using laughter, I allow myself to
experience the fun and
exhilaration of all life can be.

Resistance

Today I take a look at resistance. How do I
relate to resistance in my life? Do I shy away
from some change or challenge? Or maybe
something or someone that makes me feel
uncomfortable? This may be so; but if I
detach myself from my emotional response;
<u>I am able to embrace resistance as a tool to
help me grow</u>. My new awareness of self
evolves me to a graceful place of power.
With tools of trust, strength and courage;
I transform my resistance to emotional
freedom.

Responsibility

Today I take responsibility for myself and all that I am to my world. I choose to be fully aware of the effect I have on others, and take measures to ensure that I am sensitive, kind and mature in all my dealings with people. By taking responsibility for my feelings, my actions, and the consequences in my life, I offer myself up to be an example to others. I remove myself from stubbornness and pride that keeps me from the truth I need to see. <u>With courage, commitment, and trust I find myself to be happy to take responsibility for who I am</u>.

Self-Communication

Today I choose to look at how I start my day.
Do I wake with thoughts that are
happy or heavy? If I find they
are heavy and charged with emotion,
then I am at risk of having a "tough" day.
But if I visualise each anticipated situation
to have a positive outcome, then I am
manifesting the things that work towards
my highest good. <u>As I consciously
communicate with myself, I embrace the
happiness, satisfaction and abundant
living that I create for my day</u>.

<u>Truth and Integrity</u>

Today I am aware of the concepts of
truth and integrity. I know that without
these qualities in my life, I can feel
emotionally drained from the deceit and
dishonesty I see about me. Disillusionment
and dishonour may distort my view of my
world, but by using wholesome "gifts" of
truth and integrity, I am able to grow
stronger in my perceptual sense of self.
<u>My truth feeds my integrity; leading me to
see the virtue and honour in
myself and others</u>.

Faith and Trust

Today I recognise my need for the gifts of faith and trust. I choose to endorse them in my life, to understand their power and effect, and to know that without them I may be vulnerable and afraid.

When I have faith and trust, I feel a meaningful sense of serenity deep within my soul. Fear and insecurity disappear from my mind, and I am left with an awareness of trust that everything will work out for the best. I have faith that
<u>I am always in the right place and in the right time as I travel through my experience of life</u>.

<u>Feelings</u>

Today I am aware of my feelings. I know that strong emotions can lead me to react with a conditioned response that intensifies my situation.
My objectivity is needed to gain freedom and understanding from my amplified feelings. So today I choose to use self awareness and trust to evaluate and reform all that I feel, and to give myself gentle support to evolve into a place of emotional growth and satisfaction. I know that
<u>I am not a victim of my feelings; I am master of them</u>.

<u>Fill Up My Senses</u>

Today I experience all of my senses. I feel wonder as I feast on the delights in my world. The colours of a rainbow, the sound of birdsong, the smell of freshly cut grass, the sun on my face all fill me with humble appreciation. <u>My mind, body and soul are fed by the delights I experience while I walk on this earth</u>. As I fill up my senses, I feel a renewed sense of joy and I know that as long as I stay focused and grateful for all that enchants me, I will be happy and content. Every breath I take reminds me that I'm alive.

<u>Illusion</u>

Today I look at the illusion I choose to create
in my life. Although I see value and comfort
from all that illusion represents to me, I also
recognise illusion deludes me from the
reality of what life really is. I may be guilty
of covering up the things that most need
revealing to me. So with wisdom I choose to
disclose and discard all false areas of my life.
I find comfort and acceptance from the truth
I need to grow from. As I release illusion
<u>I embrace enlightenment</u>.
<u>I see my world through honest eyes</u>.

<u>Self Belief</u>

Today I look at my self belief. I know at times this much needed part of me is missing, causing me to think less of myself. I recognise that my perception of self is affected by my life's challenges, and so I quickly reform my thoughts to acknowledge my abilities. I know and celebrate the success of all my aspirations. Any self doubts I may have, I replace with trust. All my situations are dealt with through my confidence and assurance. <u>I need only to remember to always believe in me</u>.

<u>Sleep and Serenity</u>

Today as I lay down to sleep, I am aware of
the thoughts and feelings from my busy day
leaving my mind. I no longer feel the
emotion that keeps me from peace.
Instead I allow a deep sense of serenity to
embrace me like a soft gentle stream,
cleansing and healing me from the trials
and tribulations of my day.
<u>I surrender myself to fall into a deep and
relaxing sleep, resting myself on all levels</u>.
I move into a calm and happy state of
being.

Soul Mate

Today I experience the joy of connecting to my "soul mate". How lovely it feels to think that there is someone I am so akin to who makes my world a better place. It makes no difference to me if I know my soul mate or not, because I already feel the support and comfort of just "recognising" that our connection is there. <u>My soul mate mirrors and validates all that I am</u>, and as I celebrate our affinity, my emotions are transcended to know fulfilment, happiness and love, reminding me of how good it feels to be alive.

<u>Spirituality</u>

Today I am aware of my spirituality.
My soul feeds from the serenity that I allow
myself to experience, but complicated
feelings and emotions can lead me away
from the stillness I crave within.
So if I find myself to be misplaced
on my spiritual path, I simply change
my focus from outside to inside awareness.
Each breath I take returns me to a state of
wholeness. <u>As I embrace my spirit within,
I find contemplation, peace and happiness
fulfil my spiritual needs</u>.

<u>Time</u>

Today I am aware of time. My measurement and distribution of it can sometimes lead me to despair. I may find myself not utilising my time efficiently, or suffer the "lack" of time to be an intense pressure that causes me frustration. So today I take back my control of the situation, detach from my emotional involvement of it all, and anticipate and visualise my time working for me. As I adjust my perception of time,
<u>I relax into a knowing trust that time is on my side</u>.

<u>Visions</u>

Today I am aware of how my visions are the inspirations of my dreams. I am aware that without visions the blank canvas on which I paint my picture is without substance. Great rewards are mine as I simply visualise my life's desires.

So today I bring forth and actualise all of my visions, inspiring me to trust that great rewards can be mine.

<u>My visions are the manifestations of the rewarding reality I wish to attain</u>.

As I enjoy the bliss of abundant living, I know contentment is mine.

Be the Change

Today <u>I choose to be the change I wish to see in my world</u>. With strength and conviction I strive to make our home a better place to be. It is time for me to make a difference, and with motivation; I find myself effective in my quest to make positive changes for all to benefit. My desire to help cleanse and restore equilibrium to our world will both drive me forward and be the change I wish to inspire in others, evolving and uniting mankind to see the change they too can make to our world.

<u>Challenges</u>

Today I meet all challenges
and new projects with ease.
I am confident and able in all that I am.
I am successful in all I set out to do.
My mind and body work well for me.
<u>I embrace my personal power</u>.
<u>Everything is easy for me</u>.
I am happy being me.
Life is good.
All is well.

<u>Confusion</u>

Today I am aware of my feelings of
confusion. I know there is a need to
re-balance my sense of clarity and
understanding in my current situation, so I
remind myself to detach and stand back from
what is causing my confusion, and in doing
so <u>I give myself time and opportunity to
reflect upon my own
wisdom and knowledge</u>.
As I bring forth a much needed
sense of order and balance, I am to free to
enjoy peace, harmony and
satisfaction in my life.

<u>My Thoughts</u>

Today I am aware of any negative thoughts I may have that disempower me. How are my thoughts serving me? Am I giving away my power to negative thoughts and emotions? If so, <u>I remind myself to evaluate and reform each conscious thought to be only of positive use to me</u>. Knowing that every thought has a consequence, I use discrimination to attract only positivity into my life. As I use the gifts of evaluation and self discipline, I am empowered to be the master of my own thoughts.

<u>My World</u>

Today I hold my world in my hands, and
in my heart and in my soul.
I nourish its needs and send it love.
I embrace its full potential.
I send protection and
comfort to all people.
I am not alone as I gather strength to
unite the family of mankind.
<u>Knowing we are all one,</u>
<u>I send loving energy to my world</u>
and all who need it.
Let us celebrate our world.

<u>Pride</u>

Today I take a stand and choose to
follow my heart and my destiny. I am
able to welcome into my life a new sense
of pride and dignity. When I am
disabled by my past, or fearful of my
future, I inspire myself to have greater
determination and conviction to
honour my dreams.
<u>I am proud of who I am</u>
and with pride I step forward towards a
bright and prosperous future.

Projection and Protection

Today I feel love and energy escalate
within my own circle of light.
<u>I project loving energy as my "gift"</u>
<u>to my world and protect</u>
<u>myself from harm</u>.
Any who wish me harm will have their
energy return to them to receive
their "gift" of Karma.
Although I wish no harm to others,
I see the wisdom of the bigger picture.
Highest good for all.

<u>Success</u>

Today I am aware of my own success. I see
all my achievements as victories over
self-doubt and past failures. I am happy to
celebrate my achievements at this time in my
life, honouring my success with humble
appreciation of who I have become.
My energy is well spent as I focus on
living life to the full.
<u>My motivation and determination</u>
<u>is powered by loving what I do</u>.
My future looks great as I
continue to inspire myself to
be all I can be. Success is mine.

The Challenge of the Mirror

Today I am aware of the challenge of the mirror. Where in the reflection of others am I? <u>I realise that whatever I feel in reaction to another person is something I need to grow from</u>, and to know that all reactions I have are of use to me. I choose to be an objective observer, and to just stay interested in my reaction to others. I know that without the hindrance of my emotional response I will able to see the "gifts" in the reflection of myself in others. And so with humble appreciation, I accept and value the challenge of the mirror.

The Future

Today I look to my future with dignity and
grace. I allow myself to move forward
from the pain of my past, and with it,
all association with failure is
dismissed from my life.
I no longer need validation or permission to
feel the success I deserve.
And as I choose to follow my destiny,
I embrace all that I can be.
<u>My future brings me great rewards that
I am happy to accept</u>.
My time has come to shine.

Holistic Affirmation

Wonderful things happen to me.
I am so lucky.
I transmit positive energy.
I open myself to new opportunities.
I find solutions to all of life's challenges.
My life is good.
I am happy and my body is well.
I have lots of money, money comes easily to me.
I embrace my creativity.
I respond to my world with power and grace.
I receive reward without guilt.
I am unaffected by the negativity of others.
I use compassion to guide and protect me.
I have everything I need to be successful.
I have a clear and focused mind.
I have determination and self-discipline.
I attract good healthy relationships.
I attract love and affection.
I see my own beauty and potential.
I am safe and all is well.

Index